My Pain Woke Me Up – Legal Injustice

A Survivor's Tale of Legal Injustice in Today's Social Society

Jean Criss

authorHOUSE®

AuthorHouse™
1663 Liberty Drive
Bloomington, IN 47403
www.authorhouse.com
Phone: 1-800-839-8640

Published by AuthorHouse 12/12/2012

ISBN: 978-1-4772-8825-2 (SC)
ISBN: 978-1-4772-8824-5 (e)

Library of Congress Control Number: 2012920933

Any people depicted in stock imagery provided by Thinkstock are models, and such images are being used for illustrative purposes only.
Certain stock imagery © Thinkstock.

This book is printed on acid-free paper.

Illustrations by Dwain Esper.

Dedication

This story is dedicated to my children. As always, they continue to be an inspiration to me each and every day as I seek new creative ways to find the answers to life and its uncertainty.

My daughter is like a beautiful sunflower that continues to bloom all year long, smelling like a wonderful flower, always cheerful, and ever so precious in her own loving way.

My son is the foundation and youngest in our family tree of three; he provides the root, the laughter and the necessary bond that allows us to maintain our strength.

They both give me courage as they never truly get emotional over life's challenges, even with some of the decisions the court system made against our family. They rose above it and walked the high road, like many adults do even in their pre-teen years. I don't know many children this mature that can handle life so courageously and so well. This book is dedicated to them. I love them both so very, very much.

Poetic Justice Story #1

A few sample stories about justice or injustice as it may be

Who Steals The Goose From Off The Common

By: Anon

The law locks up the man or woman,

Who steals the goose from off the common.

But leaves the greater villain loose,

The law demands that we atone

When we take things we do not own.

But leaves the lords and ladies fine

Who take things that are yours and mine.

The poor and wretched don't escape

If they conspire the law to break.

This must be so but they endure

Those who conspire to make the law.

The law locks up the man or woman,

Who steals the goose from off the common.

And geese will still a common lack

Till they go and steal it back.

Who steals the common from off the goose?

Poetic Justice Story #2

Brainy Quotes *(a few that caught my attention)*
Various Authors – http://www.brainyquote.com/quotes/topics/topic_
legal.html

I busted a mirror and got seven years bad luck, but my lawyer thinks he can get me five.

– Steven Wright

Compromise is the best and cheapest lawyer.

– Robert Louis Stevenson

The more laws, the less justice.

– Marcus Tullius Cicero

A lean compromise is better than a fat lawsuit.

– George Herbert

Laws are spider webs through which the big flies pass and the little ones get caught.

– Honore de Balzac

People are getting smarter nowadays; they are letting lawyers, instead of their conscience, be their guide.

– Will Rogers

The trouble with law is lawyers.

– Clarence Darrow

Justice delayed is justice denied.

– William E. Gladstone

A successful lawsuit is the one worn by a policeman.

– Robert Frost

As a private lawyer, I could bill $750 an hour, but I don't.

– Jay Alan Sekulow

The good lawyer is the great salesman.

– Janet Reno

As a rule lawyers tend to want to do whatever they can to win.

– Bill Williams

If the laws could speak for themselves, they would complain of the lawyers in the first place.

– Lord Halifax

Don't let the law over-rule you! Prevail,
to your highest court!

©Marty Bucella   www.martybucella.com

"We really weren't paying attention, so based on a game of Musical Chairs, we find the defendant..."

Contents

Disclaimer

A fictionalized account of a true story

Names in this book have been changed
to protect the privacy of friends, family and business associates.

The comical illustrations were created to
capture the sequence of events in this story.

My Pain Woke Me Up – Legal Injustice

A Survivor's Tale of Legal Injustice in Today's Social Society

Overview

I know I am not the first woman who has encountered defeat, belligerence, defiance, baffling opposition, unfounded court decisions and rulings in the legal justice system. And, I am sure I'm not the first woman to question whether there is an internal brotherhood/sisterhood among "counsel" resulting in what I believe is unfair decisions, despite facts or findings. An unruly justice it may be. You have to ask is there equity and fairness out there?

My Pain Woke Me Up – Legal Injustice shares the author's experiences dealing with attorneys in the local court system, ultimately leading her to the question: Does justice truly prevail?

Prologue

Legal Injustice was written from the heart of firsthand experiences, from dealing with many attorneys and the local New Jersey court system. After a very long, tenuous divorce, I realized the courts and counsel are somewhat like a little brotherhood or sisterhood as it may be. They seem to stick together, side-by-side, and some show favoritism, prejudice, and sometimes make pre-determined judgments, before you even walk into the courtroom. Well, that's what it seemed like anyway.

They even took advantage of you knowing your health issues, especially as I was a cancer survivor undergoing breast cancer treatments at that time, and they lead your case while you were dealt the big "C" card and when you put faith in the legal system to best represent you. Later I learned, they took advantage of many with bank accounts and medical issues, and I fell prey to the system. And, it was more about driving the bus with "counsel" all throughout the process, for the best representation, whether or not you were on your death bed didn't matter, the same results could occur.

It should not matter what race, age, nationality, background, or size of bank account you have. But for some, it did. I had judges pre-assess my pleadings before they stepped into the court room, and it was a losing battle thereafter. One judge even had the nerve to say to me, *"do you know young lady this could cost you well over $50,000 if you don't come to an agreement and settle soon? Are we here to talk to about drapes?! "* She chanted.

Since I could not speak up as the plaintiff, I had to bite my lower lip, I recall. Who the hell was talking about **drapes** to begin with?! Little did she know I was already approaching six figures! Although this was not my first inclination that the judge had no clue and had not read the filing of my divorce proceedings, alleging extreme cruelty. It certainly wasn't about drapes or any of our household belongings, that's for sure. It was always about how I had been treated and what was in the best interest for me and my children moving forward. The courts didn't give a 'hoot' about me, nor the amount of time and money they cost me, and that was a dirty shame.

I know for some odd reason, this one particular judge did not care for me. Don't ask me why – it's not like I ran into her in the parking lot or anywhere else in the community. I felt discriminated against. I dressed down, nothing fashionable or flashy in court, totally tailored and professional as I typically am during business, and still she stared right at me, as though I knew her; yet I did not. I felt as if she was never going to provide me the justice I so desperately deserved. Why is that? She never even read the pleadings I found out later on from my attorney, who told me, "'They rarely do'".

"Really?" I said, "Why then do you ask us to pour our hearts out to describe what happened at great length in the legal brief, if you don't use that information?" If the court system doesn't take you seriously about what took place in the marriage, than we all might as well file under "irreconcilable differences" and have the same general court proceedings everywhere!

Well, I had the facts; you could even subpoena family and friends for that matter. I was already fighting a losing battle but by now I was in deep -- but not as deep as it got a little further down the road.

In hindsight, knowing what I know now, I may be smart enough to beat the system today, but as unjust as it seems, it just is what it is. I realized you can't necessarily disagree with lawyers, as they will keep billing you for their time. You need to drive the business decisions so the invoicing stops. Their decisions will continue to waver. It's the game they play, and they all love it as they bleed you out of your last penny, and then, go have cocktails on you!

Well, I was done after I realized I was fighting a losing battle, a game I could not win. They had won at first but now I would tell the games they played. This story will inform my sisterhood of girlfriends of the types of extreme cruelties the court put you through along with the crazy legal process. I do hope by sharing my story, my experiences will benefit someone(s)!

Legal Injustice is just about that – about how corrupt the U.S. legal system is at times; the games attorneys play; and how they prey on people during vulnerable situations. I often wondered what kind of psychology and sociology courses attorneys took in college to encourage that behavior – to get to that level in one's mind. It's a very low, cut throat way of doing business. For me, I don't care very much for lawyers these days. I've had my share throughout my life unfortunately, due to life circumstances. Only a handful of attorney's have been warm-hearted, civil, kind and sincere. It goes without saying, *"'Be kind to those who are good to you, and they, in turn will be good to others too.'"*

A friend of a friend referred me to a top-notch law firm in Morris County, supposed to be one of New Jersey's finest. This firm may have been a good one but it didn't turn out so well for moi! They had well over forty partners; *"How can there be that much business out there?"* I thought to myself.

Anyway, the day I walked into this stuffy conference room and was greeted by their team, I was offered coffee and bottled water, and then I was handed a pen and pad of paper. I sat there comfortably in this large room filled with oh so grand legalese books dating back to the 1800s!

Very prestigious indeed. *Who on earth reflected back on that old law?* I thought to myself. As I glanced around the room, twenty minutes later, the assigned small team of matrimonial partners walked in to greet me with her associate. Hello my name is . . . . and, this is . . . . , my associate(s) that will be working with you.

We introduced ourselves and became acquainted with one another. I then spent the next hour or so answering mundane questions about my background and family history to provide them with the information they needed for what was a seemingly endless process. After that my new lawyer had all the information she needed to get started, she sent me a "proposal" in the form of a legal retainer agreement with balance due upon signing.

Wow! I thought. *Cash up front please. They sure are shrewd, indeed.*

My Pain Woke Me Up –
Legal Injustice

Chapter One
Excruciating Circumstances

Yes, there were many excruciating circumstances. I was asked to think back of the personal experiences I had endured throughout my journey that brought me to this juncture, and I had to jot down relevant examples relating to our failed marriage.

The attorney's sat me down in their posh conference room, surrounded by hundred-year old law books, old enough to tell their own stories and then some. Once I gathered my cup of coffee, they sat me down and away we went. Honestly, I was wondering where the biscuits and crumpets were at these high priced fees. You see, even the initial consultation fee was an extravagant amount of money. It was about $375 I recall, to determine if I was a "worthy client." Typically something that would have been a no-charge appointment for some industries, considered a "pre-sales" assessment call. That expense was incurred for only an hour evaluation to determine if I deserved to be represented by this posh firm, known to be amongst the best in Morris County, New Jersey, or so I was told. While I was being evaluated by this firm to decide if they would "accept me" as their "new" client, I found it to be an interesting process. What actually happened was *"'Money talks and bullshit walks,'"* just like I was taught when I was a little girl. The only deserving assessment which unfolded was that my pocket-book led the way.

I was approached by a top-notch woman lawyer, a ruthless litigator, as I later learned, with thirty years in matrimonial divorce.

Why wouldn't everyone want to hire her? I thought. Well, after the first invoice, I knew why. I poured my heart and soul out to these shameless people, and mostly, all I got in return was a lot of *hullabaloo* known to most as typical *"BS"*, an uproar which started the meter ticking.

Yes, it ticked. Like a clock. *Tick, tock. Tick, tock.*

Till I then dropped with pure disappointment from the astonishment when five-digit figure bills soon started coming my way. It was utterly ridiculous. More than silly!

I felt so involved in the partnership, with a will to win and complete what I started, that all I could think about was the end result. But after months of documenting grueling example after example of extenuating circumstances, one after another, you have enough facts to build your own Fort Knox, and they just keep asking for more.

Then the court systems are so creative to postpone court dates, I pondered. . . *"Is this a conspiracy?"*

Seriously?! Are they getting a percentage or kickback from these law firms to drag things out? The billing certainly racked up! I had to wonder after they began to deplete yours and your children's bank accounts, and after I've worked so hard and long after all these years, *"Was this the plan after all?"*

Once the firm gets to see your assets the bleeding begins and doesn't end there until your assets are depleted, at least a good certain percentage.

You're no further ahead-- not satisfied with the court's outcome or with your counsel either.

So I pondered, *was this planned or contrived?* Who wouldn't think that? I was almost six-figures deep before it was time I gave this firm their very own Christmas present. I delivered their gift on Christmas Eve, and oh, what a joy it was to me. I let them go and decided to represent myself pro se till I could find the right counsel again. And then, I promptly filed arbitration for unjust and erroneous errors throughout the discourse of the marital filings. This firm never even got me divorced! In fact, they just ran up my bills to well over six figures, while I was sick with breast cancer, and just wanted to keep the billing rolling along endlessly without execution to my divorce. In fact, they claimed it would take at least another six months or more to settle – sure accordingly to their clock. For the best of the best in firms, they were a huge let-down, and I broke their so-called record of so many straight wins I suppose, since they never divorced me.

All I know is that I had a mess on my hands while I let them take the lead as any cancer patient would do, while I endured numerous breast surgeries and faced a tumultuous divorce, all at the same time.

Yes, they took full advantage of me straight away. The lead counsel was abrasive and righteous. The only person I liked there was a kind, polite, young associate. But as an upcoming junior associate, she had to follow through on directions and was exhausted, I'm sure. That was so obvious. The senior partner was like the beast and the junior associate was the sunflower child, mannerly, effective and efficient. Hopefully, this associate has bloomed and opened up her own practice by now, to spread her deserving wings. She definitely learned the ropes with my case, put in her time, logged many hours, like most good associates do.

But as I got stronger, I took over. I realized I was being taken for a ride and so was my bank account! As sad and unjust as this was, it pissed away practically a year's salary in a short timeframe. I realized, then, there was no legal morality or justice out there. The phrase 'equity and fairness' went to the wayside.

I learned on my own how to file for custody, pro se. It was not an easy negotiation by any stretch of the imagination. You might be thinking, why didn't we try mediation? Well we did but there was no discussion or room for negotiation – it was his way or the highway and I would not settle for that in the best interest of our children so I fought till I turned blue. I ended up representing myself again, two times, down the road, pro se, in court. No one teaches you these things. You just jump in and do what you know best. For me, that meant to be as prepared as I could be, like on any sales call, and have my research findings with me in court, as I did in client meetings, and hope for the best. In the court cases, you can't 'go for the close' to synch the deal. Rather, simply best represent your facts and the judge determines your actionable next steps or the best outcome, in many cases.

Well, by now, I had excruciating mental anxieties, breast pain, and had presented the same excruciating circumstances and facts from a distraught marriage that went south, very fast. All I could hope for was the best outcome and a positive one indeed.

"Do you think the court will go easy on me if I say I was abused by a parent company?"

Chapter Two
Reprieve / Remorse

As the saying goes, people can only be forgiven for their sins if they are truly sorry for their misgivings. I know this man conceded numerous times that he was sorry for what he had done but sometimes, sorry just isn't enough. The apologies in life were just too late, overdue and under delivered.

My dad always told me, *"Don't put off till tomorrow what you can do today."*

Don't put off till tomorrow what you can do today!

And that holds true for many things in life as I experienced.

Though I had good reason to put off till tomorrow, and then tomorrow, and the next day, because my children meant the most to me, and I did not want to hurt them. And then being diagnosed with breast cancer has a way of allowing the word 'procrastination' to sneak into your world as more important health issues took priority. However, it hurt me deeply that I had to break up our family unit, nonetheless, and I realized that even this old adage could hold true for personal as it did for business, so I proceeded and followed my gut and my heart.

Then, this smart law firm, on the other hand, never regretted what they did to me. No apology or sign of remorse. The only reprieve came months after I chose to take them to court, through arbitration proceedings, for all the legal mistakes I found they had made at my expense.

Oh sure, it added up all right -- from my pocketbook to theirs but it wasn't right. Then it came time for the second chance. I was persuaded to put the divorce on hold. It seemed logical at first, and yet, I was still protected legally. I needed to keep my guard up with my spouse, as I was uncertain if our failing marriage could be saved.

My new attorney told me I could put the divorce "on hold" for twelve months, and if at any time during that twelve-month window I felt strongly that progress in the marriage was not being made, I could resume where we had left off, at no additional expense and re-file. This sounded so sweet!

So I did just that. I put it all on hold to deal with my health and our marriage all at the same time – yes, it was a lot on my plate but it didn't occur at the same time. It was a big relief to table the divorce and try to make the marriage work but shortly thereafter, my diagnosis took place. Had I saved face and my marriage – one last time? This was it or the last attempt anyway. Why?! Why would one more chance make a difference now? I believed in him and us, or wanted to, at least.

The courts highly suggested the defendant participate in an upcoming recovery program which entailed group therapy for six-months in anger-management, and he actually complied. He also agreed to one date night per month with me, and I was amenable. It was better than nothing which was the way it was before. Initially, he planned all those dates, then, he stopped doing that too shortly thereafter. On occasion, he seemed fine with me going out with friends, without berating me, like he used to do before when I walked out the door and returned home in the evenings. He also accepted my job requirement of entertaining clients, which was no different from his, but as the woman of the household, it meant he would need to get home on time to stay home with the kids while I entertained on an occasional evening or two per month. He said he would travel less, help out around the home more and even take me on a long overdue vacation. What more could a woman ask for? It sounded like a perfect "fix" to our family situation. Marriage can be challenging but I was simply asking for an equal partnership in the nuptials, not an old-fashioned, traditional sided oriented, or should I say male-dominated, controlling lifestyle.

When his demeanor changed it was always easier on the children. He lifted the harsh old rules he felt so strongly about, and that I was adamantly in disagreement with, and he agreed to eliminate all cursing and derogatory language and communicate to me like a loving spouse should. He conceded to all that without the long, drawn out repercussions. At least, it was nice for about a month or so.

However, that was short-lived as the convivial drinking was back on the horizon. Even though he said he would try to drink "non-alcoholic beer" or water between his "alcohol" consumption during his business nights out and simply slow down his overall beverage intake, it was hard. He continued to return home in the unforgettable stuppering ways that I was so accustomed to. The traveling did not curtail much nor were our endless discussions about his intake, and so there we were -- back to square one.

Looking back, the first few weeks were good. But then after a month or two later, it all resorted back to the same ole. I waited of course to see if this was a short, little bump in the new system but it was not. I soon found myself calling my lawyers back and was sharing the news, *"'Let's re-file!'"* They were not surprised. They had seen this many times before, they said. If anything, they often represented women who filed twice and this process was a common thing. I didn't feel anything like a "common woman." I felt shattered.

It wasn't until two years later when I learned that this firm, again, had also taken advantage of me!

While I was settling my Qualified Domestic Relations Order (QDRO) retirement settlement two years later, I realized they dated back the end date of our marriage to the wrong end dates. I said to my next attorney, *"'Can't anyone get the facts right?'"*

He had no idea what I was talking about. Apparently, he was unaware of the first divorce filing. *"Really?"* I said! *"Are you serious, you don't know?!"* Wasn't all the paperwork forwarded on to you?

Once I brought that attorney up to speed and shared that news with him plus the large file I had, he did some investigative work and found out that the defendant's attorney had the first divorce "dropped" once I decided to put it on "hold," all without my knowledge! Wow, can this be true! *After all these years I am just finding this out now?* I thought. There were two docket numbers, or cases, not one extension? How careless of the first counsel, or was this intentional?!

I put the divorce on hold to offer my spouse a second chance with our lives together all while he was not forthright about the process. I really loved him and wanted to save the marriage after all these years to make this work for me and our children. To learn that he and his counsel seemingly omitted informing me about the dismissal of this divorce filing crucial information was extremely upsetting, and then to learn that my attorney never had the nerve to inform me either, all while I was sick I might add, was unforgettable and unforgivable to all parties involved. My law firm took full advantage of the situation with their request to "update" the divorce proceedings when I actually "rewrote" a new docket, or divorce pleading for them instead, all at my expense too. And the defendant's lawyer twisted and turned things to ensure he got a few more years on my ticket, of shared financial marital bliss. Oh what fun I found divorce to be without a pre-nup!

So while I had filed for divorce twice, at this firm's recommendation, when all I truly wanted was to give my spouse another chance to make amends, I still loved him and prayed that we could make it work for us and our beautiful children. They had suggested they could put these divorce proceedings on hold for up to twelve months, and at any time, I could resume where we left off, and pick up the docket at that time. It was less than twelve months, after I re-filed and I always wondered why I was required to "update" all those silly questions. It all made sense. The pieces came together more than two years later. You see, I later learned that the defendant's counsel had closed the original docket after I said I would put things on hold in July 2007, most likely to save face with her client (*defendant*) and for reasons of his family embarrassment.

When I finally sent the original divorce document to my current counsel, we learned that the first filing was dismissed right after I dropped the complaint by Stipulation of Dismissal filed by the defendant's counsel, without prejudice. Don't you think I should have known this information two years ago?! Everything was kept a secret from me; who was paying the damn bills? They hid the fact that the other party dropped the divorce and when I re-filed, it was no longer simply on hold.

So that was reason for all my legal costs. A smart move by this law firm (although an unethical move), I felt totally taken advantage of both mentally and financially. I just wonder how many times they had done this to other clients. How many innocent women (and men) had been told they could put things on hold, and ended up in the same boat as I? How many times had they billed, re-billed, billed for duplicate work, un-coded work, generic work that was so ambiguous that you could not dispute the billings, requested reports which went unused, subpoenaed corporate HR information when they had the identical same original documents, a minute conversation that was billed at fifteen minute intervals, and so on, and so on. It added up, that's what I know.

My breast cancer pain had not subsided but I learned as most survivors do, you do for yourself the way others do unto you. I was never brought up that wrongful way and was always doing for others but now it was time I took care of my mental and physical health and my pocket book too. So while I decided to maintain a civil and peaceful household, my law firm used the original divorce filing papers, however, what counsel neglected to tell me is that a year later your facts need to be current, and some new issue out-weighed the old. So a rewrite of the brief was going to be necessary. Wow, what an expense!

What I wasn't expecting was for this law firm, I had entrusted my soul with, to send through a bill, charging me twice to file this extension for divorce, all while they said it wouldn't cost me double!

By now I had incurred over $80,000 in legal bills, after approximately twelve months' worth of bickering, and an unsettled divorce.

While I attempted to get well; I decided to go pro se, hey!

I learned to ask more questions up front from my attorney's to try to think of all angles in preparation of our legal work. This saves time and money and expense. That's been helpful to the process but exhausting, no doubt. You pay these guys (and gals) to do the 'dirty' work for you, but in hindsight, you need to do a lot of legal 'work' yourself. In my case, it was similar to identifying the circular cause or consequences just like this old adage. . .

The old adage... which came first, the chicken or the egg?

You do the prep and they put the creative twist on it. That's all, and you better hope they do, or else you'll be back in court again fighting the same cause(s), with the same judge most likely. It's a vicious circle (a little reprise and remorse all in one fell swoop).

"He swallowed a dime? Quick, call my lawyer! He can get money out of anyone."

Chapter Three
Determination

I re-filed my case after another ten months "on hold" and was now "determined to succeed" after I realized this man's weekly behavior towards me and the children resorted to something I would no longer tolerate. I have never been so strong-willed to beat something – even while I was fighting breast cancer. I wanted the legal bleeding to end, the marriage to end, and my life to begin!

Four years later, as of New Year's 2012, it was still going on, two of those years involved the divorce from start to finish, and the last two have been with the QDRO settlement (our retirement plans). One would think we had some huge estate to settle, but instead it was because the court were so backed up, or so "We were told", and it just got postponed, and postponed. I racked up more and more legal bills as a result, and the bleeding continued. My veins are a different color now, as the red blood was all sucked away. I found errors with the QDRO and by myself, proceeded to settle pro se again. Why, you ask, since I've employed five law firms did this happen? I am still asking myself the same questions.

I have been a strong-minded, determined woman all my life. My upbringing gave me the courage to accomplish much of what I have done over the years. Now the challenge was the local County Court System and to argue for the biggest, most important win of my life – my children and my freedom to live happily and peacefully!

As I write this story, I sit peacefully in my garden on my landscaped deck -- listening to my relaxing waterfall, the trees blowing around me, green foliage sprouting in the beautiful sunshine of this spring season. The sun glistens on the porch with all types of birds chirping in the background, like music to my ears. Even the bees and the flies stop by to say hello. There was a time when I would jump at anything flying near me, but now I've learned to accept nature, and to relax around it. How serene.

The squirrels, chipmunks and even our town goffer pop its little head out from time to time as it chases the local bunnies. The deer feed from my yard, and we chase them away. It's my Garden of Eden, pure relaxation when I need a break from life's true rat race.

I've been told I am a woman of determination, one who is assertive, and I have to agree with that. I go after what I believe in – whether it is legal justice, a cause, or a person – I strive for excellence!

Perhaps it's my make-up but I was brought up on good values and strong beliefs. You can learn to cherish those values, and if you set high goals you often will achieve them. I learned to 'live your dreams,' and I do act on this in business and in my life. Some things are not taught; rather, experience is the best practice for learning something new.

I've also always been open to change. I find that being optimistic and pragmatic can help to steer me in the right direction to find my path for determination. I've had to adapt to changes many times in my life and I know that will never end. I welcome it as I do with constructive criticism. If we can't learn from our mistakes we don't grow as individuals.

If you stay focused and determined your goals will be achieved. That is what I've learned through my life experiences. I learned to finesse and navigate my way through a lot in life and found ways to pull myself above the negative and find the positive in life and the good in people.

"I made out great on the property settlement. She got the house and cars, but I got the remote!"

Chapter Four
Top Guns

You've probably heard of the top guns or the brass ring for top-notch people, programs, companies or services. Well I am one to always search for the best of the best in class, product quality and efficiency. I used the same methodology, or so I thought, with the selection of my legal counsel.

My top guns have been some of the highest ranked and best paid law firms in the state of New Jersey. I saw them flounder, and make more mistakes than marginal errors. These were grand financial errors that were at my expense, so much so it was surreal.

My high rank, low performance top guns! Yes, we are all human,

I get that. I do believe everyone is entitled to a few mistakes, here or there. But when you are paying the "big bucks", up to six figures mind you, you tend not to be so lenient and understanding of mistakes, rightfully so. And when there is a mistake, you expect an immediate apology and a correction on the books, firsthand.

I not only experienced poor customer service with my top guns once; I was now on my fifth matrimonial divorce firm and all the *hullabaloo* was not over. *PS – remember, that stands for post-settlement stuff!*

The story went like this basically: I started with a high ranked law firm in Morris County with over forty partners and I worked with the head of the matrimonial team. This firm was referred to me by another lawyer, so it came with high recommendations, and I was told that this attorney always won her cases. Six figures later, and almost twelve months later, plus two divorce filings later at their recommendation, I was still not divorced. Then, this was followed by arbitration and a marginal settlement. It was the tip of the iceberg for what I was about to experience in my newly founded *Legal Injustice*.

What I haven't told you is that this woman was very unprofessional. She dressed as though she must have bought her clothes at second hand stores, and I wasn't sure if she had bathed in months. Based on her appearance alone, I should have walked out but I did not. I kept remembering what my neighborly lawyer friend had said to me about her reputation to win cases. So I stayed on because of what I had heard and disregarded her appearance, although, I could barely shake her hand when I greeted her. Her nails reeked of dirt, as though she just came in from gardening before our court appointments, utterly disgusting. I have always been a prude when it came to business; and always taught business is business -- be professional in nature, dress appropriately, and keep personal, personal. But I always expected people in business to be courteous, clean and professional, and especially at her hourly rate, there was no reason to disregard all that in her profession!

So I was determined to make this divorce happen and decided to overlook so much especially while I underwent breast cancer surgery after surgery, radiation, and bilateral mastectomy all within the first four months working with this woman. It seemed surreal so I let "the firm" take the lead with my case and her reputation precede her. Although apparently they thought they were in charge of my "personal financial portfolio" too.

I had heard this woman was the "top gun" at her practice and never *lost* a case! Well, she broke that chain all on her own for not resolving my matrimonial matters. Then I realized they never said she never left a case *"unresolved"* or *"unclosed."* *Oh right, she didn't lose, she just didn't settle it!* I then wondered, *how many types of divorce cases she had going on like this?* How creative we can be in our world of communications? My case was the simple housewife who could not get out of a divorce. Two years later, seriously?! Locked in by ridicule, games, just absurd legal *smegaleze,* that went on and on, as did the billing.

It was right up her alley, and the other counsels, I might add. They all thrived on it. If they weren't creating chaos for their clients they were rolling the dice and playing games it seemed. This sisterhood (and brotherhood) of legal counsel was for the birds, that's what I learned. They had lost their marbles but I had lost coin! Lots of coins!!

My soon to be ex, kept saying, *"'Let's make this an amicable divorce for the children,'"* was becoming the understatement of the decade. I know I already stated this but I fired this firm's *ass* on Christmas Eve and made sure they understood the terms of that. I think they were astonished, a sickly woman like me could have the balls to do that, but I did. I had no 'new counsel' lined up but I did not care. I had worked with plenty of lawyers over the years and I knew that I could represent myself if need be. The funny thing is that it was so many lawyers due to life circumstances starting at a youthful age . . . different blends, brands and assortments; they almost surpassed my favorite cup of joe!

I would now take the time to search for the right counsel to help me get the hell out of this marriage and onto the right path for my family. The light at the end of the tunnel was so bright I couldn't stop thinking about it. *True bliss.* I knew the joy that was up ahead and fought like hell for our freedom and happiness to make that path wide open with no strings attached.

"Then it's agreed. Bob gets the car, Donna gets the house and all other property goes to the winner of a game of 'Rock, Paper, Scissors'."

Chapter Five
Stop the Bleeding, Please!

When I chose my next law firm, I did a 360-degree turn and hired a non-matrimonial counsel. He was a friend of a friend from a board that I sat on, with good local references and he lived near me in town. What more could I ask for? A soccer dad with good credentials, he seemed like an all-around nice guy, basically, a straight shooter.

As it turned out, I never compiled so much material *(legalese)* for anyone in my entire life! I dug out financial statements from fifteen years prior to create a timeline of my marriage; going back so far to prove my life's innocence and related facts. However, if this guy really knew marital law, he would have known that none of this paperwork would stand up, on a leg in court. Once you co-mingle funds, you are simply screwed; period, end of statement. I was months away from settling, yet almost seven figures deep in financial investments made during the marriage, and finding out that I could not recoup a penny was a huge blow.

Again, was this his "plan"? Did he take me for a ride too like the previous counsel? I made copy after copy of financial statements, for what purpose? I devised spreadsheets like I was becoming some sort of financial analyst, tallying up major household expenses, capital gains, stocks, joint income, and taxes, over the years, for what purpose again? I felt so invaded and then to learn that this was not going to be used in the court of law, and disregarded basically, was more than a blow to my delicate ego! I was already walking on pins and needles with what I was experiencing on the home front; my fallen marriage during a difficult time dealing with one surgery after another from breast cancer, I certainly didn't need to go through this with my hired top guns. I was in disarray – who wouldn't be?

After this mess was finally over, we settled the two-year arduous divorce and I learned that I owed more money to this lawyer, and to the defendant, and had to give him half the equity from our current home so he could buy his home, or shall I say, I paid for his new digs. The bleeding just never ended! This was the sweat equity that I had also put into our home, as my cash was liquid and his was safe in the vault, waiting for his retirement, a day I would never see.

"Your Honor, I've decided to defend myself."

Chapter Six
Pro se, Hey!

The only good news was my attorney, bless his heart, finally got me my divorce. I will give him credit for that, even though he ran up the bills like the other gal, and he made marginal errors too. I typically found more errors once I hired the next guy. It was like a domino effect.

This guy found a dozen or so errors from my first counsel. He also charged me for work that she had completed. It was a shrewd business I learned, and you needed to watch their every move they made like a hawk! When, I'd hire the next new attorney, he or she would help me find the errors from the prior counsel. Just another way to keep the billing going I suppose. It was a relentless game it seemed, and I was the guinea pig; or the dagger, and they were the arrows. What a rat race indeed!

So I finally got divorced and made a long laundry list of "to do's", post-divorce stuff, but this local guy was already celebrating on my nickel at the bank (and the bar). Yeah, he invited me, but I don't socialize with my lawyers. He had no interest in completing the real fun stuff. The list included closing on the home, handling the retirement funds, transferring the money, and the assets, implementing the custody agreement and parenting plan, refinancing the home, changing insurance policies, and so on. Yes, the biggest to-do item left was to kick this man out of my home, five months after we were divorced no less. He just would not leave! By no means was any of this fun, but this is why you hire a lawyer to help you settle post-marital disputes.

We had a difficult divorce to say the least, and I needed their help to close the deal. The defendant had already walked away, free and clear, with my cash in hand. It was what it was, and such a disappointment to say the least. Even though my attorney was tired of the attitude and behavior of both the defendant and his counsel I couldn't walk. I had a job to finish!

We finally agreed that because my attorney was in over his head, and this wasn't his area of expertise – marital law, he wanted out; I would make the transition to counsel # 3. In fact, counsel #3, an Essex County firm, found around half dozen errors or so from #2, a Union County firm, along with what I found, and the list went on. I was soon jumping around the Garden State. It was a crazy experience in a profession that should have minimal margin for error. This was the legal system for God's sake! Wasn't anyone being accurate, even with the court of law *(and we weren't talking typos!)?*

The new attorney had all this and more to handle now. He was working his lists, and oh yeah, it was fun. Did I mention that? I was miserable. While this man would not leave my home for those five months post-divorce, I heard every excuse in the world. The neighbors all thought we still had that "amicable divorce" going on while we all lived under one roof. I could not help but think that my breast cancer was going to return with the extra stress I was experiencing! I think all our neighbors must have thought reconciliation was in the works – wouldn't that have been funny! If they only knew, it would have been reconciliation #3, as they never knew about the first divorce filing to begin with, and not really the second which is why the neighbors were all taken back by surprise. Well so much for that, and that wasn't bound to happen.

No one knew of the tension between us, it was quite hard to act civil, but I still cooked dinner for the entire family (for the children of course, always for the children, not to cause any fuss, and for me and that man too!). But when he started up with his rules again, I simply put my foot down and said, all the time, I had had enough. I didn't care if he didn't like my "voice". It was over, and it was time he heard me loud and clear. Whatever games he had up his sleeve were not going to be played in my household. After all, I learned that I was no longer his "enabler" years earlier, and so I got stronger. I chimed in, spoke up, and for me and my kids and was determined to live as freely as we wanted, especially in our own household. He was now a "temporary guest" in my home until he could find his own place. Those were my rules he had to live with.

Between each of these phases I was required to represent myself during a time of transition; I went back into court 'pro se' several times for various reasons and was actually getting the hang of it. Years ago I had wanted to become a lawyer and don't recall why I never pursued that career, but now this seemed okay to represent myself, especially since I was forking over all the dough and handling this legal bureaucracy on a regular basis.

As mentioned, counsel #3 began what I called the post-divorce "dirty work"* and assisted with the home settlement, insurance, transfer of funds, set up of QDRO (though he forgot the second one – another *HUGE* error), among other miscellaneous family obligations. This was a long but important post-marital list to complete.

This man was also another nice counsel to work with at first. I always thought I found the good firms to work with but they "sweet talked" me, and ran the bills up, up and up! Matrimonial law was his area of expertise so I felt I was back on track, and my confidence in him allowed me to let him take the lead. (*Oops! There I go again. I know I should not have done that. Didn't I learn yet? Not to give these lawyers cart blanche? I guess not*).

His associates were turning over like pancakes and making one error after error.

All I know was that I was briefing them left and right, and getting billed for the work I submitted. What were they doing? It sure was

costly. If I'd attempt to discuss those billing matters with him, the main partner got confrontational, abrasive and defensive with me. He'd throw some legal jargon at me and try to intimidate me. I wouldn't budge – after being through what I had, I was tough as nails. Not exactly the courteous or professional demeanor I was taught from most professionals I had worked with, that's for sure. Who did they think they were, or were trying to impress? Was their legal strategy to attempt to belittle their clientele? Well they picked the wrong lady.

After all was said and done, I thought I paid a pretty hefty fee, and always on time as well. This attorney just kept hitting me up for more and never was satisfied so he decided to take me to arbitration court and I let him for some unfounded reasons. He made a foul of himself in my opinion, and brought this huge binder in for the arbiters that apparently may have impressed them. I went in pro se, prepared with my timeline and facts, and unfortunately did not come out ahead. The legal injustice just continued! That internal brotherhood/ sisterhood was staring right at me from around that conference room table – the arbiters and my former counsel were in partnership together it certainly seemed, they all sided together. There was no righteousness whatsoever!

It was almost humorous as my former counsel even thought he had me on trial that day – for real! He was drilling me believe it or not, instead of just stating his peace of mind like we were both asked to do. Wasn't he on my side previously representing me just months prior? I wasn't in a court room arguing against him rather just there to settle a darn billing dispute, for goodness sake. It's unbelievable how they operate! They walk over you and stomp on innocent people, and try to wager their law degree in the courts eye while the babe in the woods has no leg to stand on, then you bleed to death.

There went another five grand and I'd be sure not to recommend this guy to anyone. In fact, the nice business colleagues of mine who did refer me to him couldn't believe this story when I told them. Well his channel of referrals ended I'm sure. What they don't realize is that they cut themselves off at the foot, and do it to themself.

I decided since counsel #3 made various errors on numerous things and I would handle the paperwork, I let him and his associates go and once again, successfully closed on my house. It was ridiculous and so time-consuming and complicated with our financial situation. Then I hired counsel #4, I believe a Passaic County firm, which now seemed like I was jumping around the Garden State again. Where were the money trees? I was becoming broke and so I got creative and went to Employee Assistance Program (EAP) through my health insurance plan. After all, I was paying through the roof for these benefits, why not utilize them?

Counsel #4 was a nice old gentleman. He took the case but about two months later, he came down with a health issue and could not continue on; he wasted some time and caused more court delays. I was now in search for counsel #5, and this wasn't over yet!

I went back to EAP and got another referral -- another great law firm in Morris County. This man shared some personal stories, saying he was retiring soon, and all I could think about was . . . *"Please, please just get me out of this mess and finalize everything, then you can go retire, and play golf as much as you'd like!"* And, here we are.

Counsel #5 was unprepared as we prepped the night before the arbitration hearing so I thought to myself, why pay this top gun and his nice young associate the big bucks when I don't feel confident they are going to win? Come to find out, they did not win that day either. No matter what angle, the arbiter's minds were made up, well in advance it certainly seemed. Almost as though they decided before we walked in the door!

Ever since I signed another retainer agreement though, it was just like co-mingling your funds again in marriage, meaning, pay-up or get out. I know they didn't mean that but that's what it felt like to me, another blow to the ego. Although they were the kindest gent's to-date and seemed the most reasonable, it was my legal injustice for not "winning". They acted on most my requests and seemed to follow a logical legal process but the legal injustice never quite ended. The court simply ruled against me, not in my favor, once again, greatly, to my chagrin and disappointment.

Today, I am still with this top gun although I am jumping back and forth representing myself pro se on certain issues in court, depending upon the project scope and the effort required for each initiative. A client should not have to "shop counsel" so many times like we do for cars and clothing these days. These unnecessary steps cost taxpayer's time and money and the court systems too!

I consulted with various other lawyers from time to time to keep this firm on its toes and, on point; so of course, I obtained second and third opinions regularly. In many cases, I thought I was right and they were wrong with the findings. But who's to judge, it's only money – mine, and time, right?

It's been difficult to bear and the outcome after continually being let down. I've learned to accept that *"Winning does not define success."* Success will come from completion at the end of the rainbow. In my case, my rainbow has not been finalized yet. The colors have not been drawn out completely. That's the way I look at this situation. I know that someday, hopefully soon, it will be over, but I have prepared myself mentally to handle it in the present while it has not settled. My colors look good, and I have way passed that half circle mark on my rainbow, thankfully. That's the best I can do while I support my children and fight like hell for our freedom and rights as a new family unit.

And these have been my top guns – almost $200,000 later, ludicrous right? For a fifteen-year marriage and now going on a four-year divorce (two years pre-divorce/two-years post-divorce) with wasted time and money indeed.

It's been tough to stay in the driver's seat while being dealt the cancer card during this entire ordeal as well but somehow I've managed to persevere, and find the pursuit of happiness.

"I haven't worked in weeks. We're having personal problems and he's only talking through his attorney."

Chapter Seven
The Retainer Agreement

I learned in my early life about these agreements -- by definition, a "retainer agreement" is a binding agreement in which a fee is paid to retain services from a lawyer. The options of a retainer agreement are as follows;

A) A sizeable payment is made up-front, left in escrow and billed monthly

B) The bill is paid at settlement

C) The client is billed monthly for services rendered

Most firms prefer Plan A. Plan B was a win/win, as no money is required up front; the Plaintiff only needs to pay up when a settlement is reached. Typically, thirty-three percent (33%) is awarded off the top, less expenses to the firm. Yes, they win a sizeable portion since they 'float the bill' so to speak, it's often a given. Plan C would be great if you could control legal expenses. In most cases, it's out of your hands. They charge as deemed fit. Every fifteen minutes rolls up to thirty, thirty to forty-five, thirty-five to forty-five, forty-five to sixty minutes, and so on. It's an expensive propaganda and I know they know that!

I think in law school attorneys are taught "it's all about the billing" rather than "the good intentions of winning and good will of your client." That's how I feel anyway.

So now let's spend time and discuss Plan A, the most popular retainer agreements. I had several. They include parents, grandparents, siblings, next door neighbors, office supply companies, the gamut. Well just kidding but that's certainly what these things felt like. Billing for everything but the kitchen sink!

Senior partners billed at $425/hour while associate partners may bill anywhere from $225 - $375/hour; legal assistants charge @ $150/hour; and the list went on. Yes, I told you I had hired top guns and was certainly paying top fees! What I realized is they had thrown everything but their cleaning bill on this monthly invoice and found a creative spin to bill me for it. These were non-descript invoices, of course, and with many generalizations, so it became extremely hard to dispute the bills for time and material, or effort.

I became wiser and savvier with each growing day. But one thing I knew, taking on the legal system was an uphill battle. Whereas writing about it (the good and the bad), on the other hand, has been a piece of cake!

www.martybucella.com

"Sorry, but I don't make a move without first consulting my attorney."

Chapter Eight
EAP Resources

I decided to bring in the top guns from the Employee Assistance Program (EAP) – a business organization to assist those that need financial or legal advice, healthcare assistance or personnel/HR consultation as an objective third-party resource, I had used EAP in the past to select marriage counselors and now decided to go this route as a smart, low-cost alternative to help resolve the post-divorce issues.

I mentioned the first EAP attorney was a very nice old gentleman, counsel #4, a good hearted and smart man who took ill. I think they were all smart but this was the mundane stuff that needed full-time attention to bring to closure. I don't blame anyone for parking my file on the back seat. However, at $350 plus an hour for any of these guys I had high expectations that they would deliver what I requested in a timely manner.

When I went back to the drawing board at the EAP organization in search for yet another attorney; I was not only more cautious with my selection, I interviewed them as though they were going to be a future employee of mine, and didn't really care what they thought. The tables had turned and it was my turn to "assess them" to determine if they were worthy of me as their client!

Yes, I got bold, and rightly so. This new boutique firm fit the bill and that's all I really cared and as an added plus, they practiced all forms of law – so it fit the bill, and they could represent me with all sorts of mundane matters that I had to get through, thankfully.

So this nice man and his very small team (#5) were hired, and slowly we started to accomplish bringing my case to closure, but I never lost a beat and kept my eye on pace with them. I didn't like doing this but it was now my job to see to it that what I wanted got accomplished. I was in a healthier place in life and beyond most of my breast surgeries and could deal with the legal bureaucracy now. I was past the divorce sand was just handling all the custody and parenting issues, QDRO and post settlement stuff for the most part. I'm sure this isn't how everyone needs to drive their business with lawyers, but after my personal experience I had all the reason to do this and more, so I did.

I just felt like I kept choosing the wrong firms, with strong referrals or not, one after another. I had learned those referrals didn't mean a hoot in the end, who knew?

Chapter Nine
Ditch the Debt

In all my years of sales from high tech to media sales, I had never seen such a long "sales" cycle. The time it took to close my divorce was unheard of. I had sold multi-million dollar technology deals which they took far less time to negotiate and close than this silly divorce! Many celebs took just a week or two for their high-profile divorces to settle, in what seemed to be in the public's eye, and for far less dinero. Now, I am no celeb, but I certainly felt like one with the bills I was receiving from all sides of the system.

The courts allowed this process to drag out. It was a dirty shame, and the process was over managed and under delivered by all. It all was so crazy (and expensive I might add). These delays cost money, caused a lot of aggravation on both sides, and increased the animosity between the plaintiff and the defendant. Our once "amicable" relationship was thrown out the window and had become a desperate one filled with frustration, aggravation, and despair.

I never understood 'why, when, or how' this happened to me, but I did learn to accept the 'what and where' as it became my day-to-day reality. My kids were old enough to understand it all now too. We learned to watch our spending throughout the divorce and especially after I got sick but that, too, put pressure on the marriage.

All I wanted was to "Ditch the Debt".

So I learned from a girlfriend who was involved in non-profit and real estate to express myself through charitable work. Although I had been involved in various fundraising since my teenage years, I learned later in life about non-profits.

Charity work can be self-fulfilling, but the only thing it doesn't do is pay the debts! I realized I could fundraise as much as I'd like, and as good as giving back felt, what I needed to do was simply to pay my bills. They would not take care of themselves so I got creative. I put my inner creativity to work, and unleashed profound thoughts and inhibitions. I let my mind take me to new territory, to where I have not gone before. If blessed, you can do this now, and good things will come your way. Someone once told me,"*A goal is simply a dream with a deadline.*'" I just loved this quote! I lived by those kinds of rules and loved it! I followed my heart and my inspirations, and learned to live by my dreams (my next book).

I told myself this over and over again, and lo and behold, it worked! Elation began. I started writing my second book, and third, and designed and patented a product (something I had been passionate about for quite some time), obtained a licensing agreement to produce other multi-media products, and away I went. I unleashed those inner thoughts, utilized my sales and marketing experience I had gained over the years, forgot about my past and the negativity that I had heard over and over again, and put that knowledge to work to 'Ditch the Debt.'

I had incurred more than my share of loss during these years of turmoil. I endured pain, heart break, and many other kinds of loss (true love, breasts, and money). My reward was waiting to happen. I was ready for it and was going to make it happen! The debt and legal bills would be gone very soon. I would see to it! My determination took control.

If I didn't take this attitude I would throw in the towel and give it all up, and that was not going to happen. Especially not now!

New Video Game
Space Invasion: Attack of the Attorneys

Chapter Ten
Legal Injustice

I sought proper counsel to resolve the remaining outstanding issues but it never came to fruition. I often wondered, *"'Was there a legal brotherhood in the justice system?'"* Some things just did not seem right.

Why on earth could I not get closure on the QDRO, two years post-marital divorce? Why was it so hard to wrap things up? It took three law firms and over $xx,xxx in additional legal fees, and counting, for simple processing of retirement paperwork, a standard post-divorce procedure. Also, why did it take the first two firms so long to get me divorced the initial hefty amount? Two years later, from start to finish, plus well over $xxx,xxx. Well, as I mentioned, I was not some high flying celeb, known to throw money out the window on frivolous things. They had figured out which buttons to press for a short while, while I was under the weather, but now I pressed the buttons and, in fact, my conservative upbringing taught me to be smart about financial planning and spending, as I had succeeded throughout my entire life.

I always budgeted and paid bills on time, kept cash on hand (thanks Dad for all your good financial tips!), bought things only when we needed them. Invested wisely and knew how to grow my financial portfolio, year over year.

Dad taught me several lessons about *"'Money talks and bullshit walks'"* and, *"'Don't put off till tomorrow what you can do today.'"* Always good advice. There were too many days though when I came across those with the alligator arms, that didn't dig deep into their own pockets, and expected me to dish out the coin.

As example, I only shopped for clothes quarterly for me and the kids and bought incidental things in between, as an example of how I watched our spending. I used coupons and was not ashamed to do so, I shopped during sales; there was nothing wrong with a good sale! But I also paid full price for something nice that I really liked – that was how we were brought up with the finer things in life. I am not a wasteful person either, rather, I was taught to be kind and generous – *"'So, I did unto others the way I would want them done unto me'"*, as the saying goes!

Now I was dealing with a legal system that barely would hear my side of the story before making their minds up prior to us (plaintiff & counsel) sitting down in court that day.

Does this really happen? I guess so. My lawyers certainly agreed.

They were well prepared – facts, research, examples, case studies, all in hand, and yet, we never got anywhere that day.

Or, perhaps, was someone being paid off? Now I know I am not be the first person to dislike the outcome of a court hearing, or the last, nor am I one to make false accusations, but I was always taught that perception is reality – and this was my reality!

What in the world was going on here? I thought. All I know was there was no legal justice for me. A lot of uncertainty – yes, a lot of expense – yes, a lot of stress – yes, a lot of time – yes, and lawyers, legal bills, retainer agreements, court fees, plus extra legal costs – yes, yes, yes!!!

My list grew and so did the *legal injustice*. I went back and forth to represent myself pro se in hopes to resolve certain matters on my own. I do believe my pulse made a difference in court and I lit a fire under a few butts. However, I still don't know why the system was inept as it was, and I doubt I will ever know why.

I took other's words of advice and it wasn't enough. I tried to rush to the finish line – life's lesson. Do your research. As I learned with my breast cancer options, lawyers are no different. Research their success, their failure rate, and pending cases if you can obtain that information. Speak to referrals, not just the ones provided to you. Do not go based on personal references alone, no matter how well trusted those personal colleagues and friendships are. Those people most likely do not know any better than you. After all, they are probably just friends or neighbors and have never hired them or ever been involved in a legal matter, so who's to judge but yourself.

Legal injustice exists. Be aware. Stay clear, if you can, and run like hell to higher ground to stay ahead of the curve!

I learned to focus on my strengths and to put those to work, as Marcus Buckingham, a great business author once taught me, 'How to manage your StrengthFinder?' From how to manage around weakness, to how to manage a person strong in communication, context, deliberative, discipline, fairness, empathy, harmony, futuristic, ideation, input, intellect, positivity, self-assurance, and in the woo, among others. I built on those strengths and rebuilt my confidence at home and in life overall and decided;

Don't let the law overrule you! Prevail to your highest ground!

That is my only advice. Perhaps one day I will understand the indifference that occurred; maybe I can make change for the better, but if not, you will be aware. And I know I am not the only one who has experienced *Legal Injustice* in their lifetime.

Poetic Justice Story #3

POSTED IN:

Lawyer Faces Possible Discipline Over Epic Christmas Poem About Never Ending Divorce Case, Above The Law, 07 May 2012 By Staci Zaretsky

http://abovethelaw.com/2012/05/lawyer-faces-possible-discipline-over-epic-christmas-poem-about-neverending-divorce-case/

A.Todd Merolla, Merolla & Gold, represents Drew Doscher in a divorce action that has now been litigated for more than a decade. Can you say "divorce train wreck"? Apparently the judge who had formerly presided over the case died in May 2011, and several motions had been pending since before his death. This really ticked off Merolla, and prompted him to write the poem in question, which began rather innocuously:

ALL I want for Christmas is to finally get my Divorce

Subj:**A Christmas Poem and a Letter**

Date:12/23/2011 1:36:42 PM Eastern Standard Time

To:xxxxxxxxx@courts.state.ny.us

Cc:xxxxxxxxx@aol.com; xxxxxxxxxx@kjwlsw.com

Twas the week before Christmas, in the Matrimonial Park,

All the creatures were stirring, putting their horse in front of the cart,

The fee applications were pending, bills demanding to be paid,

In hopes that Drew's resolve, soon would fade.

The attorneys and consultants nestled all snug in their beds,

While visions of paid fees danced in their heads.

The Good Ship Lollipop continued on an unchartered map,

They all settled their brains for a long winter's nap.

When down in the basement there arose such a clatter

They sprang from their desks to see what was the matter.

Away to their computers flew like a flash,

To bill Mr. Doscher in hopes of some rest.

"Good luck getting a trial date," former counsel would scream,

"Make him pay me another $173K," Mr. Weinstein would dream,

Don't forget my repairs; they were in great need,

Ten toilets in five years, not excessive, there's no greed.

The Honorable One now passed, who will take the torch?

To rule on pending motions, some two years on the porch.

Justice delayed is Justice denied,

Will Article 78 inspire someone's pride?

Win, lose, or draw, it's not for a judge to care,

Simply rule and move one, why is that such a dare?

This 2003 case be a 59-month marriage, 9 year divorce,

$1.5MM "temporary" maintenance to-date, can Plaintiff get more? Why, of
course!

In October of 2007, His Honor more than one time declared,

"It is the expeditious trial of the matter, which you know I'm all in favor,"
you know that I'm fair.

Yet twenty seven days over seven months in '08,

He claimed to have not enough data to deliberate.

Then two years later, when ready for the mini-trial,

His Honor sent the matter over to JHO O'Connell

Upon review of the record, and arguments far and near,

No new evidence to benefit Plaintiff would ever appear.

Was the exercise futile? It would certainly appear so,

Some nine years later, Drew must keep paying, so it continues to go.

"What's your number?" "Make a business decision," they all insist,

With nary a reference to the marital estate, yes. We get the gist.

The first time around Drew heard Miranda 3 or 4 times on the stand,

Warned that criminal action would soon be at hand.

"You had better settle," said the Powers to Be!

Else we will tell the District Attorney and the SEC!

These accusations turned out nothing more than a bluff,

Akin the wolf that would huff and puff.

One lesson learned these last 9 years is quite base,

It's illegal for a lawyer to threaten criminal action to settle a civil case.

Those in Brooklyn learned the hard way,

'Round the same time this Plaintiff said Nay'.

Before using process as a weapon, one better must think,

As those in King's County found themselves in the clink.

So back to the math class, we must go,

Everyone bring their pencils, be their rain, wind, or snow.

This time it should be fair, everyone play it straight,

Do it according to the Constitutional Mandate.

$2.77MM was not enough to cut it this week,

Already paid $294k, Mr. Weinstein is looking to wet his beak.

Fees, fees, fees, they think at some point will be too much to bear,

But Mr. Doscher is still standing, not going anywhere.

Tis the season for giving and to be jolly,

There must someday be an end to this folly.

A Final Judgment of Divorce be entered, whether fair, wrong or right,

Merry Christmas to All, and to All a Good-Night!

Poetic Justice Story #4

EXIT RAMP

My Day in Court

Another hapless defendant learns about our legal system the hard way. BY MICHAEL J. SCHNITZLER

9:30 AM
I arrive at Tinton Falls Municipal Court 10 minutes late, but confident, with a stack of documents in hand. Two months earlier I was issued a ticket for "use of handheld device." Yes, I was holding an iPhone in my hand while driving—but it also happens to be an MP3 player, which I play through my car speakers.

I did my research and found the relevant law, which states: "no phone, texting or use of communications" while driving. I printed it out along with my phone and text records to show that I was not communicating at the time I was ticketed. I was ready to defend myself.

The courtroom is packed with at least 400 people. I take my place among the standees.

All eyes are on the man enthroned above us in his black robe. In front of the judge stands an intimidating-looking sergeant in a smart uniform, his face frozen in a half-frown.

With brisk gestures and terse commands, the judge conducts the room like an orchestra. Opening files like so many musical scores, he quickly sizes up each case.

"Sir, you're aware of the charges...?"

"You can settle it in court today for $750, or you have the right to an attorney...."

One hapless defendant after another is strong-armed into filling the city coffers. The judge clearly enjoys his job. I am getting angry.

10 AM
I find a seat.

10:30 AM
Someone's cell phone rings. The sergeant completes his frown.

11 AM
I'm starting to get hungry.

12 PM
A smartly dressed young man stands. He doesn't have that defeated, submissive look.

The judge is visibly agitated. He pronounces the terms. "Pay $900 in fines today and avoid possible suspension of license." The smartly dressed guy wants to say something, but the judge cuts him off.

"Trust me, this is what you want!"

Nausea wells up inside me.

1 PM
There are about 100 of us left. The judge is working faster now.

I hear bits of dialogue.

"Work it out with the prosecutor."

"$250 surcharge."

"$35 court fees."

My hands are getting clammy; my mouth is dry. I'm starting to rethink my strategy.

1:03 PM
The judge walks out. We are warned not to leave.

1:36 PM
Hearing my name, I walk to the front of the courtroom and take a seat near a hulking police captain. He examines my file, runs his hand through his hair and looks up at me.

"There are no points for this ticket. why are you here?"

I answer weakly. "I'm not guilty."

He looks at me quizzically.

I explain about the MP3 player.

The captain whispers something to the prosecutor sitting beside him.

The prosecutor declares, "That's also illegal."

I try to protest.

Eyes bulging behind metal glasses, the prosecutor cuts me off. "You're arguing with me?"

The sergeant comes over to see what's going on.

They all look so well fed.

The prosecutor continues, "You could wait for the judge to come back, plead not guilty when your turn comes, then get a trial date, spend another day here, and if you lose you'll have to pay double the fine, plus $250 and court fees."

My heart races. My stomach rumbles. The energy is draining out of me. I prepare to speak. The captain gives me a wink. "Come on Michael, it's just $130. I'll walk you to the window."

1:59 PM
I am beaten. ✳

Michael J. Schnitzler is a freelance writer based in Lakewood.

My Pain Woke Me Up – Legal Injustice   55

Poetic Justice Story #5

Kelly Rutherford Breaks Down on 'The View' Talking About Custody Battle. ABC News, By SHEILA MARIKAR, 09/13/2012

http://abcnews.go.com/blogs/entertainment/2012/09/kelly-rutherford-breaks-down-on-the-view-talking-about-custody-battle/

Kelly Rutherford broke down in tears on "The View" today talking about her custody battle with her ex-husband, Daniel Giersch, who lives in France and was given custody of their two children, ages 3 and 5, late last month.

"It's just been crazy," she said, wiping away tears. "My little girl said 'I want to come home mama, I want to come back to New York. 'My son, who's kind of been brainwashed, says where he is is so much better." . . .

ABC News legal consultant Dan Abrams appeared on the show with Rutherford and called Judge Theresa Beaudet's Aug. 28 custody decision shocking. His commentary about the ruling is headlined "Two American Kids Shipped to France in One of the Worst Custody Decisions. Ever."

Kelly Rutherford Vows to 'Never Stop Fighting for My Children', PEOPLE Magazine. By STEPHEN M. SILVERMAN, 09/01/2012

http://www.people.com/people/article/0,,20626382,00.html

Locked in an international custody battle since she and Europe-based ex-husband Daniel Giersch divorced in 2009, Kelly Rutherford refuses to give up the fight – even after a judge on Tuesday ruled that the *Gossip Girl* actress's schedule is flexible enough to allow her to travel back and forth to Monaco to visit her two children.

"I will never stop fighting for my children. They're my babies and they're very young and this is going to affect them profoundly and I want to be there as much as I can to show them that this isn't my fault, this isn't something I wanted, and that's my concerns,". . . Rutherford, 43, said on Saturday's edition of ABC's *Good Morning America*.

In court on Friday, Rutherford's request for her kids – Hermes, 5, and Helena, 3 – to be brought back to her in New York while she appealed Tuesday's legal decision was denied.

. . . "I'm all for 50/50 and all for children having a mother and father and co-parenting – it's just that the way it's set up now – I'm a working mother," said Rutherford on the TV program.

"I've been the sole supporter of my children for their entire life. . ."

A Touching Story

A dear friend once shared this story with me, and I'd like to share it with you.

A young lady confidently walked around the room while leading and explaining stress management to an audience with a raised glass of water. Everyone knew she was going to ask the ultimate question, 'half empty or half full?'... She fooled them all.... "How heavy is this glass of water?" she inquired with a smile.

Answers called out ranged from 8 oz. to 20 oz.

She replied, "The absolute weight doesn't matter.

It depends on how long I hold it.

If I hold it for a minute, that's not a problem.

If I hold it for an hour, I'll have an ache in my right arm.

If I hold it for a day, you'll have to call an ambulance.

In each case it's the same weight, but the longer I hold it, the heavier it becomes." She continued, "and that's the way it is with stress. If we carry our burdens all the time, sooner or later, as the burden becomes increasingly heavy, we won't be able to carry on."

"As with the glass of water, you have to put it down for a while and rest before holding it again. When we're refreshed, we can carry on with the burden - holding stress longer and better each time practiced.

So, as early in the evening as you can, put all your burdens down.

Don't carry them through the evening and into the night... Pick them up tomorrow. *(Thanks Susan!)*

1 * Accept the fact that some days you're the pigeon, and some days you're the statue!*

2 * Always keep your words soft and sweet, just in case you have to eat them.*

3 * Always read stuff that will make you look good, if you die in the middle of it.*

4 * Drive carefully... It's not only cars that can be recalled by their Maker.*

5 * If you can't be kind, at least have the decency to be vague.*

6 * If you lend someone $20 and never see that person again, it was probably worth it.*

7 * It may be that your sole purpose in life is simply to serve as a warning to others.*

8 * Never buy a car you can't push.*

9 * Never put both feet in your mouth at the same time, because then you won't have a leg to stand on.*

10 * Nobody cares if you can't dance well. Just get up and dance for God's sake.*

11 * Since it's the early worm that gets eaten by the bird, sleep late.*

12 * The second mouse gets the cheese.*

13 * When everything's coming your way, you're in the wrong lane.*

14 * Birthdays are good for you. The more you have, the longer you live.*

16 * Some mistakes are too much fun to make only once.*

17 * We could learn a lot from crayons. Some are sharp, some are pretty and some are dull. Some have weird names and all are different colors, but they all have to live in the same box.*

18 * A truly happy person is one who can enjoy the scenery on a detour.*

19 * Have an awesome day and know that someone has thought about you today.*

AND MOST IMPORTANTLY,

20 * Save the earth..... It's the only planet with chocolate!*

About the Author

Jean Criss is the author of a three-book series, **My Pain Woke Me Up – Bliss, Legal Injustice,** and **Live Your Dreams** *(due out in 2013).* The trilogy is a fictionalized account of a true story, documenting many of the author's life experiences, lessons, and best practices learned along the way.

Jean is a recognized sales and marketing innovator in the digital media industry with more than twenty five years' experience, and currently, devises creative sales and marketing solutions for clients while collaborating on many levels across a variety of media platforms. Before the launch of Jean Criss Media LLC, Jean served as a leader in the Northeast and Midwest markets for various publishing and technology companies, where she gained her digital-media expertise and built ongoing relationships over the years.

Jean works with various non-profit organizations in her community lending a helping hand by fundraising through corporate sponsorships, by serving on their board, and by being a passionate advocate for their organizations. Most recently, she was appointed to the Summit Fortnightly Club (FNC) publicity chair board, a local women's organization that fundraises for community-related charities.

Jean is a key leader for the New York franchise, Ladies Who Launch (LWL), a women's entrepreneur group coaching women in business to "Dream it, Launch it, and Live it!"; and Believe, Inspire and Grow (B.I.G.), a newly formed community based women's entrepreneurial organization headquartered in New Jersey. She recently joined inspiring organizations such as 100W (OneHundredWomenMakingADifference.com) and 6-Figures.com – this program makes entrepreneurship accessible to any woman with a project, dream or aspiration to start her own business or simply live her passion. Other industry memberships include NY Women in Film & Television (NYWIFT), Cable Advertising TV Bureau (CAB), and dozens of local community chambers throughout the region.

Jean lives in northern New Jersey with her two teenagers. She is writing her third book in this trilogy series entitled *My Pain Woke Me Up – Live Your Dreams*. A story about entrepreneurship; how to dream big, live your dreams by unleashing your inner creativity and making your dreams come true. She designed and self-published her trilogy series, drawing upon her multi-media experience from writing, creative design, publishing, and marketing.

"Believe me, I have plenty of experience with cases like yours."

A special thanks to my new friend, Marty Bucella, Cartoonist/Humorous Illustrator, who allowed me to add a little more humor to my story.

Now I will *Live My Dreams* and Eat Some Chocolate!

(Stay tuned for the last inspiring book in this trilogy series
about how Criss launched as an entrepreneur,
how she unleashed her inner creativity by focusing on the positive,
to develop digital media and other product platforms from the
ground-up,
and focused on the right people,
and the important things that inspire her to Live Her Dreams).
Release Date 2013

The End